HOW TO SUCCEED IN

AFFILIATE MARKETING

Disclaimer

The sole intention behind writing this e-book is to provide information. We have done everything we can to ensure that this eBook is accurate and comprehensive. But there can be typographical errors or material. Furthermore, the material in this e-book is only valid as of the publishing date. As such, this eBook ought to be regarded as a reference rather than the final word.

This eBook is meant to be educational. The content in this ebook is not guaranteed to be accurate by the author or the publisher, and they will not be held accountable for any mistakes or omissions.

Regarding any loss or damage caused or claimed to be caused, either directly or indirectly, by this eBook, the author and publisher shall not be liable or responsible to any person or entity.

TABLE OF CONTENTS

Introduction

Among the best online income opportunities for anyone is affiliate marketing. This is a fast, passive, highly scalable, and simple to set up way to make money. Not a technical
While expertise is needed, you might quickly make hundreds or even thousands of dollars if you select the correct products and target the proper market.

But first, let's take a little look back. To begin with, what is affiliate marketing exactly?

And why is it so much more successful than other online entrepreneurs' money-making techniques?

But first, let's take a little look back. To begin with, what is affiliate marketing exactly?

How does it operate? And why is it so much more successful than other online money-making techniques?

Business owners?

Affiliate marketing is essentially selling a product that isn't yours in exchange for a commission. After that, you get paid for each sale you make, so all you have to do is link that item.

when speaking to a willing audience.

HOW TO SUCCEED IN AFFILIATE MARKETING

Selling affiliate goods like eBooks will frequently allow you to keep 70% or more of the sales! If you select the appropriate product, you can make the same amount of money as someone who constructed a product on their own.

You will discover the advantages of affiliate marketing in this book, along with tips on how to get going quickly and profitably. With a well-chosen product, an eager audience, and just a tiny amount of luck, this has the potential to truly transform your life.

For individuals who are currently offering affiliate products, this guide ought to furnish you with the extra abilities and strategies required to genuinely elevate your enterprise.

This also applies to the implements.being utilized by leading companies to market BIG ticket items such as powerhouse computers that cost $5,000 or more and MBA courses.

Many people are confused by the concept of affiliate marketing. How is it possible to profit from the sale of something you didn't create?

How is it possible to make money online so easily?

It can be simply explained as basically being sales. You are taking on the role of a vendor and getting paid a commission for each sale.

You are similar to the door-to-door salespeople who arrive circling to pitch you broadband.

The distinction is that you are not knocking on people's doors. Your door is the internet, and through it, you can access everyone on the planet.

You immediately gain a significant edge from that, particularly if you figure out how to entice people to visit you.

There will also be a significant variation in the commission structure in this case. Typically, regular salespeople receive a meager 5–10% percentage of anything they sell. As previously stated, the

HOW TO SUCCEED IN AFFILIATE MARKETING

The distinction with affiliate marketing is that you will receive between 70 and 80 percent of the sales. That's correct: you will frequently make more money as an affiliate marketer than the product creator does!

Because you can start making money just like you would if you were selling your own product, but without having to invest a lot of money, affiliate marketing is quite alluring.

Creating funds to start something from the beginning.

Furthermore, you have the option to select a product that is already selling well because you will be marketing an existing item. When you make your own goods to market, there are

There's always a chance that what you create may be unpopular.

That is considerably less likely when you just market something that is very well-liked

The scalability of affiliate marketing is yet another fantastic advantage. You can begin making money from an affiliate product within hours if you build a single webpage promoting its benefits.

What would prevent you from creating a new page to market a different product in that scenario? And another page to market an additional item?

How Affiliate Marketing Works?

Now, shall we go a little more technical? What is affiliate marketing exactly like, and why would a creative ever be content to part with so much of their own earnings?

Let's start by thinking about the kind of content you plan to sell.

Affiliate products will be perceived as digital goods by many marketers.

Numerous other choices exist, which we will discuss in this book.afterwards. But we'll concentrate on it for the time being. This includes items such as presentations, online courses, and eBooks.

As digital products have no overhead and no "COGs," or "cost of goods sold," as it is known in business, they are an excellent option for online sales right away. Thus, it follows that the

The creator can just make money and split it with the customer rather than having to pay out for each sale.

HOW TO SUCCEED IN AFFILIATE MARKETING

It is therefore likely that the creator used Word or a camera to create this digital product themselves, or they may have hired someone else to do it. In either case, they'll have created this e-book or course with the goal of making a profit by selling it.

Subsequently, the creator most likely started selling the goods on their website or through an unrelated web page. They'll make an effort to increase website traffic as much as they can encourage customers to purchase from them, and they will generate a passive income of their own.

However, an individual can only exert so much influence before their resources run out. At that point, a creator may begin searching for affiliates to collaborate with in order to aid in the promotion of their goods.

It also implies that they are spared from having to manage delivery or make significant upfront financial commitments.

HOW TO SUCCEED IN AFFILIATE MARKETING

In order to encourage us to promote their items, the product designer is thus willing to give affiliates like us 70% and more. Additionally, they want us to promote their products rather than those for which other creators are offering affiliate schemes.

Even though the creator will only now receive 30% of the sales, this is still 30% more than they would have received in the event that they hadn't left.

And that seller will be generating enormous profits—much more than they could on their own—if they can entice thousands of people to their books with a horde of internet marketers.

This is a win-win situation, to put it briefly. By inviting marketers to collaborate with them and help them reach a thousand more sales, the inventor

They can profit just as much from their own eBook or course as they would if they had to create one and take that big risk.

To be more precise, this process is carried out through the use of "affiliate links," which function through cookies.

You will be provided with an affiliate link when you select an affiliate product to market, which you must put on your sales page and in your blog entries.

A buyer will be taken to a different website page when they click on your affiliate link. Here, a cookie that identifies them as coming from you will be saved on their machine. Right now,Affiliates get to keep the majority of the sales while selling a product as though it were their own!

What Is Affiliate Marketing

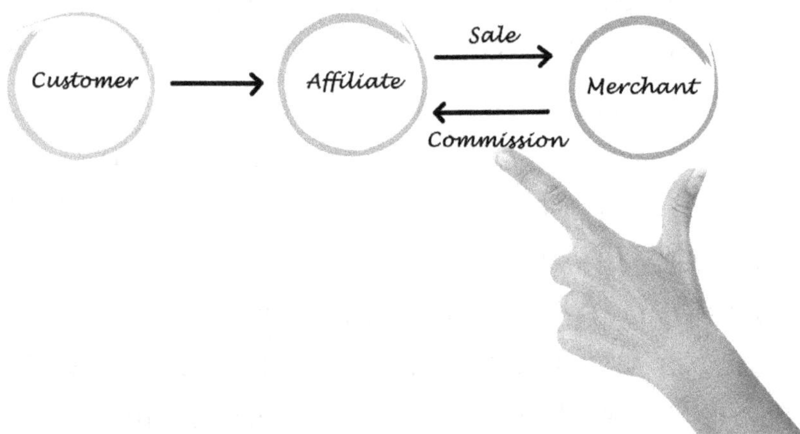

They will be identified as "one of yours" when they make a purchase from that store, and the commission will be added to your account so you can withdraw it at a later time.

It's easy for you to do: just give the URL and advertise the product. That is the only step involved!

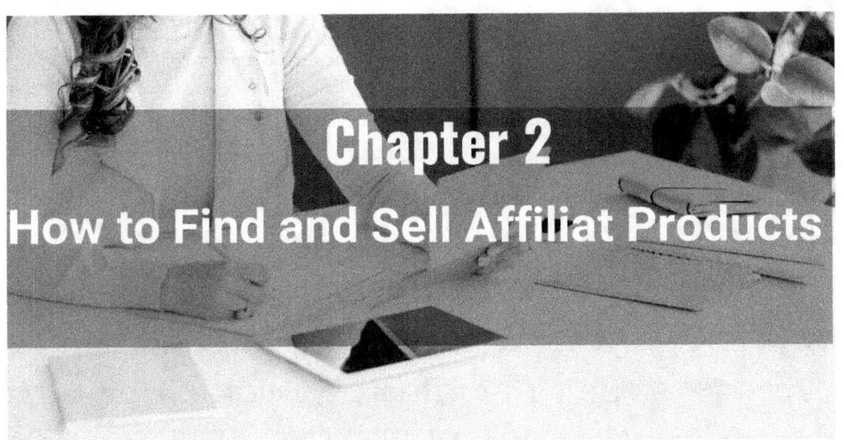

Well, enough with the speculative chatter. How can one actually begin their journey as an affiliate marketer?

You will, however, require a product first. To obtain this, you must will need to visit a website like Commission Junction or Clickbank. JVZoo is another excellent one.

This page offers you access to a wide range of products with affiliate programmes. Simply scroll through to find the ones that catch your eye.

HOW TO SUCCEED IN AFFILIATE MARKETING

You may notice some details about the various products, so make an effort to look for the products that give a respectable commission and are selling for a fair price.
Certain websites allow you to view an approximate amount of sales, in which case

Naturally, you want to search for the products that are selling well.
You must get in touch with the product's owner after deciding which one to promote. You can utilise your link as you see fit once they give it to you in the event that you are successful.
However, it's also important to remember that a lot of affiliate products come with marketing materials.Keep in mind that your success indicates the success of the creator. They will frequently provide emails, a sales page, banner ads, and other materials because they have every incentive to see you succeed.

HOW TO SUCCEED IN AFFILIATE MARKETING

It is highly recommended that you select a product that gives these kinds of advantages if you are a novice to the world of marketing. This allows you to quickly get started by just copying and pasting the available resources.It is highly recommended that you select a product that gives these kinds of advantages if you are a novice to the world of marketing. In this manner, you can start moving.

almost immediately by just copying and pasting the available resources.Then, you ought to see that you are selling in the same quantities—the product and the marketing copy are the same. Thus, there's no reason why it shouldn't function equally effectively.

As I previously stated, this business model is essentially a "copy and paste" one. You're just imitating the system used by someone else who already has the product selling successfully.

Make certain that the money will go into your bank account

Selling Physical Products and Services

Although selling eBooks on websites like JVZoo is a great approach to guarantee that you may keep the whole profit, it is not without its drawbacks. Contrary to what some other marketers may claim,Physical products continue to be the most common category of products sold online.

And when you give it some serious thought, this makes sense. What percentage of people do you know who purchase tangible goods? Almost all of them, I believe? However, how many individuals do you know who would purchase an ebook?

Granma doesn't know how to utilise a PDF file, therefore she might not (unless it's through Kindle). In the same way, your non-reading friend most likely wouldn't either!

You essentially get a significantly smaller portion of the market as a result.

What is the process for selling tangible goods as an affiliate marketer? The most favoured choice is to join the Amazon Associates programme.

A lot of marketers find Amazon's associate plan, which is their take on an affiliate programme, to be a really alluring alternative.

Researching affiliate marketing will probably lead you to discover that the great bulk of it is devoted to digital product sales via platforms like Commission Junction, JVZoo, and ClickBank.

HOW TO SUCCEED IN AFFILIATE MARKETING

Things are not the same on Amazon. Amazon can't normally give you more than 4% or maybe 8% at most because they already divide the profits with the producer, have to pay for storage, shipping, and postage.

This implies that in order to make a reasonable profit, you'll need to sell a lot more goods at a lot higher price.

Does that imply, however, that you should disregard Amazon Associates? Not at all.

To begin with, selling tangible goods is frequently far more profitable than selling digital goods. Consider this: are you more likely to spend a lot of money on something you have to read on a computer screen or something you can hold in your hands and show to friends?

Even better, people trust Amazon as a firm and are familiar with its brand. They can purchase with just one click, so they have a far higher chance of doing so!

Other Options for Selling Physical Products

Since Amazon offers such a large selection of things, almost every article will have a suitable companion piece.

Lastly, you continue to get paid even if a user clicks on your URL and purchases something else from Amazon! This has the potential to yield substantial profits if someone were to – for examplepurchase a new computer, for instance, and receive 8% of that amount.

HOW TO SUCCEED IN AFFILIATE MARKETING

You would still receive that fee even if you didn't actively advertise the product—as long as you directed the customer to Amazon in the first place.

The best course of action, then? Employ both affiliate marketing strategies! Just remember that if you exclude Amazon from the picture, you will lose out

You will learn in later chapters how to maximise the benefits of Amazon products by promoting them in a slightly different way.

Amazon in the UK. Amazon.com still allows you to sell things, but all you can do in return is get vouchers.Directing a vendor or manufacturer who does not have an affiliate programme is an additional choice. and to see if they would think about making one for you. If you are successful in doing this, you may be able to negotiate an exclusive contract and earn a sizable commission as well.

Naturally, in order for this to be effective, you must be able to prove that you have the authority and clout to justify their time.

Selling Services

Selling a service or an SAS (Software as a Service) is an additional choice. This could be the most profitable choice!

This is because a lot of services may present you with a reoccurring commission.Suppose you are successful in persuading someone to register on a gaming website.

Certain online casinos provide a percentage on all sales made by that client for the duration of their association with the company!

Similarly, you will frequently be offered a commission that is paid to you each month that the person you persuade to sign up for a hosting account or other recurring service with would receive.

Naturally, the commission may be little at first. BUT, it may then accumulate to a significant amount of time. You may have hundreds or thousands of conversions in a few years, which

then continue to bring in money for you even if your website went offline!

Affiliate marketing is a very easy and successful technique to generate money online, but it is not infallible. In other words, if you select the incorrect product or promote it improperly,

It's possible that you won't experience the kind of quick success you were looking for.

Your ability to select the appropriate product will therefore be crucial to your success. What you should know is as follows.

What Not to Sell

When selecting a product to sell, the majority of individuals first load their preferred affiliate network (ClickBank, JVZoo, WSOPro), then search for the products with the highest sales and the best commission.

This is a wise decision because the numbers imply that if other people are making a lot of money, you should too.
Their business concept is actually "copy and paste"able!

However, if that's all you're doing, you're not doing it correctly. 99% of the products at the top of the ranking will all focus on three specific topics: dating, fitness, or generating money online.

You will now be in competition with everyone else selling that book as well as everyone else selling books that are comparable if you start advertising one of those books. The majority of users who have been online for

We've already had enough of being pitched "make money from home programmes" for more than a day.

Furthermore, they are the online niches with the highest levels of competition. If you don't already have an incredibly popular website or email list, ranking first on

It will be nearly impossible to Google "Build Muscle" or "Make Money Online eBook." You are positioning yourself for failure.

Alternative Strategies

Alternatively, think about selecting an item from a narrower niche. Let's imagine you come across an eBook targeted at a certain field or occupation, such as one that explains how to sell flowers online.

organising. The market is smaller and it feels less thrilling, but your product is now distinct.

Furthermore, by leaving comments on a few flower blogs, you can effortlessly connect with those flower arrangers. Additionally, you may most likely rank your sales page higher on Google for the phrase "flower arranging eBook."

without difficulty. Additionally, it has a distinct USP that makes selling it very simple.

Even better, though, is to consider your current marketing channels. Which connections are you able to use? Where are a lot of folks who you can reach? What interests those individuals?

Before choosing the product, consider where you will reach your target audience and how you will sell it. That's how you get ahead and it's a tactic you can use again and time again.

It makes sense for you to select a product that will appeal to your audience if you already have a popular website with a sizable following.

Multiple Products

Additionally, keep in mind that you have the choice to sell a large number of items. Another significant benefit of selling digital goods is that you may easily add or remove items from

without having to dedicate days to writing and formatting for your website!

Multiple product selling has benefits and drawbacks. If you have a large website and are utilising soft-sale strategies, selling several things is fantastic (see the following chapter). This also enables you to charge various rates to various kinds of customers.

Having said that, concentrating on only one product at a time can enable you to generate greater interest in and buzz about that one particular product as well as a more efficient website that takes users to all to the buy page, a single page.

Choosing Physical Products

Selecting tangible goods involves a rather different procedure. Once more, the goal should be to choose items that are pertinent to both your content and the average website reader.

They should also be high-quality products that meet actual needs at the same time.

The good news is that there's no need to take a chance by purchasing a large number of things in bulk at a high upfront cost. You won't have to deal with a scenario where your warehouse is filled of many spinning toys for distraction!
This implies that you can chase trends and, in general, try a lot of different things and see what sticks.
To appeal to all types of customers, I would advise you to offer a variety of products at various pricing points.

However, keep in mind that you get paid a commission for any purchases made once the consumer visits Amazon. This indicates that encouraging the individual to click the link and visit the page—possibly even more so than marketing that particular product!

####

Create your website and get a web host. Create a new page and include your affiliate link and the sales page copy that you have. Now that everything is set up, you can begin.

Sell and begin to turn a profit! In the next chapter, we'll examine this next stage.

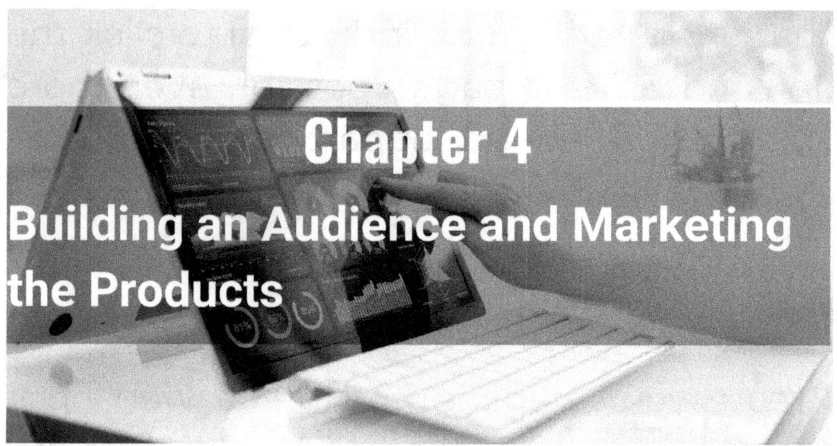

Building an audience before selling affiliate products is the secret to success. The "catch" (if there is one) is that it requires you to genuinely invest some time and labour to achieve the highest sales figures.

The good news is that you will effectively be making a lot of money for doing something you enjoy if you choose an intriguing topic. However, you must first develop that following and earn their trust as an influencer in order to reach to this position

Exist any further avenues for affiliate goods sales? Naturally, of course! And this chapter will also cover those. However, I still strongly advise you to grow that following and ensure that Individuals are drawn to your brand.

How to Create a Brand That Sells

Naturally, gaining this kind of influence is not simple. It takes a lot of work and dedication to get to the point where people will purchase items simply because you promote them.

sincere effort to gradually deliver true value The first step in doing this is building a website and a significant social media following. Instead of trying to close deals straight immediately, take your time developing that loyalty and trust by running a campaign of providing content of consistently high quality.

What matters most? Possess a distinct, powerful brand, a compelling goal statement, and a tangible "buyer persona." (The buyer persona is a representation of your "perfect customer"

The biggest error is attempting to design a website that appeals to as many people as possible in a very general way. Just like with the digital product you initially purchased, this tactic may not work.

The reason for this is that, when you go too wide, your brand will inevitably become boring and uninteresting.

For example, a "fitness" website is too general and overdone to be widely used. It entails facing out against the entirety of the internet. What distinguishes you in a crowded market?

Instead, think about creating a website about fitness for people over 40. Consider Paleo Fitness instead. or Cross-Fit. or Exercise Outside. or Extreme Bodybuilding

Each of these choices has a more intriguing hook, a mission statement that is lot clearer, and a target demographic that is much clearer. Each of these will appeal to fewer people overall, but those that do,will be far more inclined to interact and show excitement that there is a product available just for them.

Then, this distinct and fervent objective ought to be the source of the brand. This implies that a person should be able to tell right away whether they will find your logo or website design appealing to them or not. Your content should support your brand's clear communication of who it is for and what it stands for.

The website for bodybuilders who are serious about their sport will probably have a lot of dark, muscular men in red and black with articles on "boosting testosterone with compound lifts."

The paleo fitness website, meanwhile, is probably going to be white and green with pictures of people running in the outdoors

From this point on, everything you do—including your social media posts and advertising—should align with this picture. Subsequently, your affiliate product selection have to target the identical demographic. Additionally, you'll sell it using that value proposition and market it in that manner.

It's also essential that you offer fresh, original information that shows genuine competence.

This may come as a shock, but you will never sell the affiliate product if you employ a writer who is ignorant of the subject. Why?

Since the hired writer's only ability is to investigate the subject and repeat it using their own language.

This implies that none of the information will be novel or insightful, and it may even be outdated or erroneous (since they won't be familiar enough with the subject to recognise when this is the case).

Either compose it yourself or work with a writer who has a sincere interest in the subject. Why? Since they will then be able to discuss something BRAND NEW and ENTertaining! Here's how one becomes a

thought leader, and persuade others to join up and listen to you since they're seeking a fresh viewpoint.

Show courage. Make a difference. Show a lot of passion. Next, pick a product that appeals to the same market.

Not enough time for that? Rest assured, there are alternatives. additionally things are mentioned below.

Placing Your Link

It is quite simple to sell as an affiliate marketer. You get one link, which you can use to promote a product. From there, you can publish that link wherever and earn money.

Thus, the question is: where should it be placed?

The majority of us will usually post our link on a sales page or landing page, however this is not the only choice. We'll examine how it operates in this section along with a few other options.

Creating a Sales Page

A webpage on a website that has been created expressly with the intention of making sales is called a sales page. This implies that it won't offer any more content, such as articles, and probably won't other links or even advertisements. Anything that can potentially divert attention away from the goods you're selling shouldn't be here.

A sales page will typically have a very long and thin layout, which will entice users to scroll down and take their time reading what you have to say.

Must admit.

They will feel as though they wasted their time, which makes it much more difficult for them to leave without making a purchase!

Writing, though, is what matters most. If you craft your sales message effectively, you may convert this captive audience into willing customers.

Writing persuasively has the potential to transform you into a marketing guru. You are not looking for these drones.

In the end, you will be considerably more successful at making sales, getting people to subscribe to your list, and overall accomplishing any goal if you know how to utilise words to persuade an audience.

you're trying to find.

So how does one acquire this superpower? These are some helpful hints.

•Attract attention:

People don't want to go through lengthy texts because they are rushed. The first step in persuading your audience is to get them to really read your written comments. How are you going about this? Making a strong statement at the outset is one strategy.

Another is to employ a narrative structure to draw the audience in. The latter is very effective since, by nature, we find it very difficult to stop reading a story before it ends!

• Use data and facts:

Since they haven't met you and are aware that you are trying to sell them anything, they aren't always inclined to trust you. Alternatively, allow the statistics to speak for you.

Your case will be stronger if you can cite more sources and figures from more authoritative sources.

• Anticipate:

Make an effort to foresee the worries that your readers might have and address them straight away. You could say, for example, that there are "several beautiful sounding

online' but emphasise that it's not "just another scam."

Reduce risk:

"Loss aversion" is a basic human tendency. This indicates that they would prefer to hang onto what they already have than get something new. You must

eliminate all danger by providing free trials and money-back guarantees.

The most crucial thing to do is comprehend the value offer. Your product's emotional appeal is on your ability to make readers believe that it will transform their lives.

For instance, in the event that you should be aware that you aren't actually selling an eBook on fitness if you are selling one!

The feeling of having endless energy, toned abs, and a tonne of confidence is essentially what you're selling. You must pay attention to that!

Try to evoke a feeling in the reader by speaking from the heart; ideally, it will be enthusiasm for purchasing your goods.

Recall that a lot of digital items include pre-made sales pages similar to this one, so all you have to do is buy the script wholesale and put it on your own page.

All you have to do now to start producing conversions with your sales page is to point your audience in that direction. You can accomplish this by promoting your goods on your emails and

social media. You can even include product advertisements elsewhere on your website, such as in the sidebar.

Building a Store

You may create a store to sell your affiliate products from if you are selling numerous of them, which is also a really smart idea. This implies that you'll be emphasising and advertising items that are appropriate for your business, similar to what you might find at an online retailer.
The buyer will now be directed to an external page instead of your item when they click on it, which is the only noticeable difference.

This can be easily accomplished, for instance, by utilising the WooCommerce e-commerce plugin, which is compatible with WordPress.

This will enable you to establish a store on your website where customers can able to see the goods. It allows for affiliate content, so when a user clicks on an item, your referral link will direct them to the new page.

More Ways to Sell

However, what if you included links in the body of your articles?

Although not many affiliates use it, this is a fantastic way to monetise a blog or website. Just pen a piece about

Choose a topic you want to write about, then include an affiliate link in the content. In this manner, you can gently advertise the product, and anyone who is interested in your material might click it.

It works similarly to adding AdSense to your page, but you get to actively urge users to click the link and make a lot more income. You may even be truthful that it brings in money for you.
cash!
In fact, you are required by law to disclose that you are earning money from those things in a lot of places throughout the world.

Making use of a plugin that appends a message to the bottom of each page on your website, but remember.

The top ten list is one of the finest content formats for affiliate product sales. If you work in the fitness industry, you can write a countdown post that lists the top home workout equipment, or you can develop

If you write about technology, you should produce an article listing the most powerful laptops available.

on any case, this is an excellent way to drive traffic and revenue. It also works well for rich snippets, which are a great way to make your material stand out on search engine results pages (SERPs).
Similarly, there is no restriction on your ability to include an affiliate link in an email's body. Reaching people directly in their email at a moment when they could be open to your message is a terrific method to extends.

eBooks can also contain affiliate links. To your PDF, you can add links if you are offering a digital product for sale or free download. It is likely that those who are reading this are very interested in

and hence more inclined to purchase what you suggest. Since these are qualified leads, it's the ideal setting for attempting to close sales of even more expensive goods.Imagine earning a lot MORE money from everyone who reads the book and takes your advice than from selling a digital product for $20 a pop.

Alternatively, what about including an affiliate link on a printed flyer or pamphlet? Using a simpler, more memorable URL and having it reroute to your affiliate link is the ideal method to implement this. In this manner, you can genuinely make in-person product advertisements!

These ideas serve in part to show that you don't always need to be aggressively marketing the product; you can try the soft-sell strategy of just including the link, maybe along with an image.

This is particularly effective for tangible goods (particularly when a well-designed button is used and the product is directly tied to the page's content). If your website is well-known and receives a lot of traffic

Having a tonne of content, then just putting buy links in there can result in a tonne of sales gradually coming in. and the total of them is!

You just need to be inventive to use affiliate links in a variety of other ways. Try a variety of things and experiment; you might be surprised at what works best for you and your product!

PPC Advertising and Other Marketing

What happens, though, if you have no audience? What happens if your readers don't trust you as an influencer?
In this scenario, you'll need to figure out how to direct people to your straight from the sales page. The good news is that PPC (Pay Per Click) networks like Facebook and AdWords make it simple to accomplish this.

With pay-per-click advertising, you only have to pay when a user clicks on your link. You determine the maximum amount you will spend "per click" as well as the budget's cutoff point.

Your ad won't appear when there are a lot of competing advertising from other firms in the same niche if you set your per-click cost too low. If you set it too high, you probably won't make any money.

You can choose the audience to whom your Facebook ads are displayed depending on the data individuals disclose on the social media platform.

These consist of:
- **Age**
- **Sex**
- **Location**
- **Hobbies and interests**
- **Job title**
- **Income bracket**
- **Interests of others**

And more!

The goal of using AdWords to place adverts on Google is to take into account both the intent of the user and their interests (depending on the "keywords" they are searching for).

individual.

PPC takes intent into account because it indicates if a user is looking to buy or is just conducting research.

If they are doing research, they may look up the "best computer games of the year" online. If they intend to purchase, they may hunt up "cheap computer games" or the name of the game online.

You can also employ "negative keywords" to exclude terms (like "free download") that could imply a user is not interested in making a purchase and is acting improperly.

Ensuring that consumers ONLY click the link if they are likely to make a purchase from you is the goal of pay-per-click advertising. This raises the possible profit while lowering your expenditure.

Thus, the advertisements have to be "targeted" as precisely as possible to the proper audience, even if it means scaring off potential customers with the right language.

Naturally, the link should send visitors to a sales page to increase revenue. Next, you should pay attention to your website's conversion rate. Put differently, if the writing on your landing page is strong, then 1% of visitors may convert, which would mean 1% of visitors make a purchase from you. The more you can afford to spend on advertising and yet turn a profit, the higher this number is.

Direct Selling Through Facebook and Other Platforms

Naturally, one of your other options is to sell straight through those other channels. Nothing prevents you from posting an affiliate link in your Instagram bio, Facebook group, or

as soon as the swipe-up feature for stories is added). If you lack the time or ability to design a website, this is a good approach to develop a loyal following.

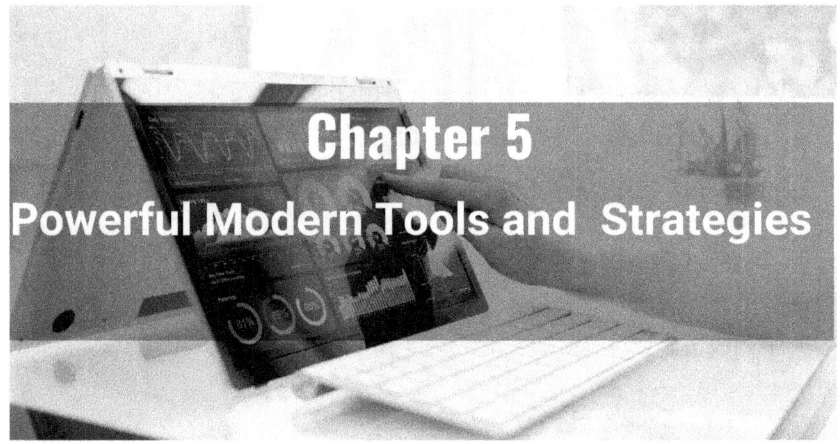

Offering a variety of goods, such as digital, services, and physical goods, is significantly more effective since it combines the kinds of enormous sales that may be made by developing a devoted customer base. audience with the VOLUME that comes with moving a large number of tangible goods.

Another thing to consider is that you have the choice to include items that are "pie in the sky" sales because you have such a wide range of affiliate products to offer on your website.

For instance? I once used an affiliate link to sell an MBA! This was made possible by EDx, an affiliate network with enormous potential for profit program, though also an example of one that you must sign up for.

The difficulty? balancing and overseeing so many disparate things!

Because of this, the major, established companies will employ technologies that simplify this procedure and provide them with access to some of the most profitable online affiliate networks.

Crucial Tools for Taking Affiliate Marketing to the Next Level

Genius Link is one such tool. You can join several different accounts and then add their affiliate programmes using Genius (https://www.geni.us/). This functions

especially well with Amazon, since it lets you add accounts to all the various localised versions of Amazon.

You don't have to worry about losing clients because each link will direct them to the appropriate version of Amazon depending on where they are. Additionally, you can add several other programmes.but also places like iTunes, BestBuy, and Barnes & Noble!

From this point on, creating a link from Amazon is as simple as copying the sales page's URL and entering it into a box.

Assuming you have the Chrome plugin installed, simply click that button moment the website is viewed in your browser! Trackonomics(https://www.trackonomics.net) is a comparable choice. Similar functionality is provided by this programme, but it allows you to add things from a far bigger list of affiliates.

This covers products such as the previously mentioned EDx. Even better, Trackonomics enables you to look for products across a wide range of affiliate accounts and then select the one that generates the highest revenue most money.

You don't have to worry about losing clients because each link will direct them to the appropriate version of Amazon depending on where they are. Additionally, you can add several other programmes.but also places like iTunes, BestBuy, and Barnes & Noble!

From this point on, creating a link from Amazon is as simple as copying the sales page's URL and entering it into a box.

Assuming you have the Chrome plugin installed, simply click that button moment the website is viewed in your browser!

Trackonomics(https://www.trackonomics.net) is a comparable choice. Similar functionality is provided by this programme, but it allows you to add things from a far bigger list of affiliates.

TThis covers products such as the previously mentioned EDx. Even better, Trackonomics enables you to look for products across a wide range of affiliate accounts and then select the one that generates the highest revenue most money.

put it another way, if you are selling a smartphone, you can now compare the fee you would receive if you sold it directly to Amazon versus from Amazon. directly from the producer. Compared to Best Buy and all other available options!

In order to determine which of your links is the most popular, to determine when a link is down, or to determine how much you have made in a certain period of time, you may also use both tools to track clicks and transactions duration.

The sole drawback?

The monthly fee of Trackonomics is ALMOST $500. However, a free trial is available. In the interim, Genius Link is free.

More Tools

Although there are many more alternatives available for individuals who wish to construct a more streamlined business strategy and funnel, these tools will help you increase your affiliate profits to a whole new level.

For example, using Google Analytics is nearly necessary to monitor the effectiveness of your website and particular pages.

You can check your ranking for various phrases and make those improvements phrases, and then observe which routes generate the highest commission and how those pages link to the sales page.

Comparably, you can also refine your landing page to the point where it significantly boosts conversions by utilising tools that enable you to do A/B testing on it.

Conclusion

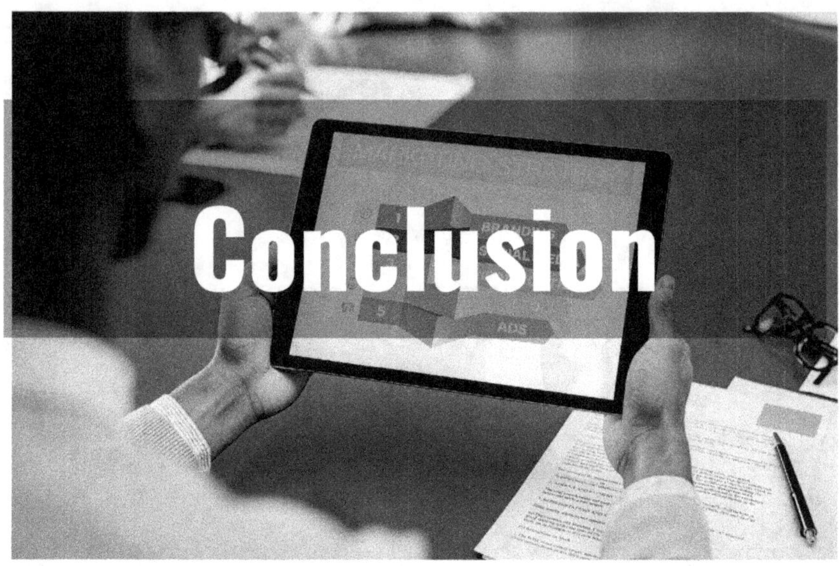

That brings you up to date on all you need to know to launch a lucrative affiliate marketing company. It's up to you whether you keep things simple or reach for the heavens, but I strongly

Advise you to take the guidance in this book and attempt to sell actual goods with a wide market and high prices in addition to the conventional digital eBooks and courses.

The classic process for selling affiliate products is simple:

- **Find digital product and get an affiliate link**
- **Create a sales page**
- **Place link on sales page**
- **Send traffic to sales page both from your own website, and through marketing**
- **Wait until the product stops selling, then rinse and repeat**

It is my suggestion that you make a small modification to this model in order to increase revenue and create a longer-lasting, more robust business plan.

Here's the new strategy:

- Establish a website and cultivate a following of people who like and trust you.
o Do this by producing genuinely original and passionate content.
content that has a clear mission statement and visual brand

Select a few high-priced affiliate goods and services, make sales pages for them, and then "launch" them from your website utilising hype-building email blasts and teasers.

o Identify the best-performing products, then use paid advertising to drive more traffic to them. · In the interim, sell as many smaller digital products, physical goods from Amazon, and services as you can through articles and websites that you optimise for search engines.

You may now enjoy making money while you sleep, no matter what you do! The more you try new things, the more effective your sales approach will be!